THEORY IS FUN

GRADE 4

Maureen Cox

First published 1988
by **Subject Publications**

Revised 1990
New edition 1994
Fourteenth impression 2015

Copyright © Mimast Inc 2015

ISBN 1 898771 01 4

Printed by Pardy & Son (Printers) Ltd.,
Parkside, Ringwood, Hampshire, BH24 3SF

Tel: +44 (0)1425 471433
Fax: +44 (0)1425 478923
Email: sales@pardy.co.uk

For my son Stephen

★　★　★　★　★　★

If you are aiming for higher grades in music or greater understanding when listening to music, you need this book as a stepping stone to Grade 5 theory and beyond.

This book builds upon the theory of the first three Grades in the same simple, direct way. There are illustrations for fun and you will again find a crossword puzzle, a wordsearch and other means of testing yourself. All the musical terms for Grades 1 to 4 are in the dictionary at the end of the book. On the last page is your own record of progress chart.

With my help you can take your fourth step towards Grade 5 and still enjoy the theory of music. With this book you will again find that Theory is Fun.

MJC

Acknowledgements

I am grateful to the many Professional Private Music Teachers and Members of the Incorporated Society of Musicians who use *Theory is Fun* with their pupils and I should especially like to thank Alison Hounsome, Christina Bourne, Brenda Harris, Alison Hogg, Judith Homes, Ann Leggett and Marion Martin for their very constructive comments and helpful suggestions.

Maureen Cox

CONTENTS

KEY SIGNATURES

At Grade 4 level you will be expected to know **major** and **minor** key signatures up to and including 5 sharps and 5 flats. You must know the minor scales in their **harmonic** and **melodic** forms.

All the key signatures you need for Grade 4 are on page 7 opposite. You have already met most of them.

Remember to place the sharps and flats on the correct lines and in the correct spaces.

Special Note

The A♯ is placed in the bottom space in the bass clef, not on the top line. If it were placed an octave higher, then in the treble clef it would be on a ledger line!

Major and Minor
Key Signatures

major	key signature	minor
C	no sharps or flats	A
G	F♯	E
D	F♯ C♯	B
A	F♯ C♯ G♯	F♯
E	F♯ C♯ G♯ D♯	C♯
B	F♯ C♯ G♯ D♯ A♯	G♯
F	B♭	D
B♭	B♭ E♭	G
E♭	B♭ E♭ A♭	C
A♭	B♭ E♭ A♭ D♭	F
D♭	B♭ E♭ A♭ D♭ G♭	B♭

Test yourself

Name the keys

___ major   ___ major   ___ minor

___ minor   ___ major   ___ major

___ minor   ___ minor   ___ major

___ minor

Teacher Check Time

page 8

THE ALTO CLEF

The alto clef is also known as the **C clef**. This is because **middle C** is found on the *middle line* of the stave.

It is printed like this ↘

If you wish, you may write it in other ways:-

The important thing is that the two curved halves of the clef should be drawn either side of the middle line of the stave.

In former times the alto clef was found a great deal in vocal music.

Nowadays the alto clef is mainly used for the viola.

Test yourself

Name these notes.

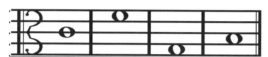

Write these key signatures in the alto clef.

B major   F minor

Rewrite the following treble clef passage
in the alto clef, keeping the same pitch.

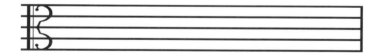

Teacher
Check Time

SCALES

Now you have reached Grade 4 level, I shall assume that you understand the differences between the harmonic and melodic minor scales.

There is a new scale for Grade 4 - G♯ minor. This scale uses a 'double sharp'. The double sharp is necessary because you have to raise the 7th note in minor scales and in G♯ minor the 7th note already has a sharp!

What will you do to raise the 7th note of a minor scale if it already has a sharp?

Replace that sharp by a double sharp.

The Double Sharp

A double sharp [✗] raises a note one tone. Here is the key signature of G♯ minor:

To remind you of their differences, here are both G♯ minor scales, using double sharps.

G♯ harmonic minor

G♯ melodic minor (ascending)

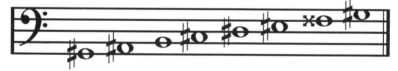

G♯ melodic minor (descending)

Test yourself

1. Write **_with_** key signature in the **_treble clef_** the scale of D♭ **major** **_ascending & descending_** in **_minims_**. Mark the semitones with ⌐.

2. Write **_with_** key signature in the **_bass clef_** the scale of **G♯ harmonic minor** **_ascending & descending_** in **_semibreves_**. Mark the semitones with ⌐.

3. Write **_without_** key signature in the **_treble clef_** the scale of **G♯ melodic minor** **_ascending & descending_** in **_semibreves_**. Mark the semitones with ⌐.

If you are working through this book on your own, it might be a good time to ask your teacher to check your scales test.

You might have made a small mistake which you have not noticed.

The Double Flat

Now that you have mastered the double sharp, I shall introduce you to the double flat. It looks like this:- ♭♭

When placed in front of a note, it simply lowers that note one tone →

TECHNICAL NAMES

Each note of the scale has a different *technical* name. You have already met the **tonic** - the first note. Each note is also given a *Roman numeral*.

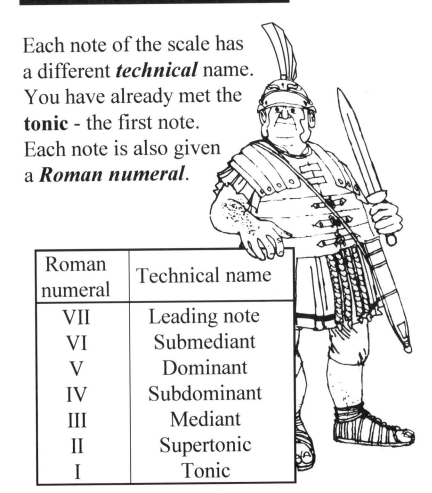

Roman numeral	Technical name
VII	Leading note
VI	Submediant
V	Dominant
IV	Subdominant
III	Mediant
II	Supertonic
I	Tonic

How can you remember these?

Technical Names...

One way to remember the
order is to make up a
sentence. For example:

Two **S**peedy **M**otorists **S**low **D**own **S**eeing **L**ights

Now you make up   L_____
a sentence ↘   S_____
                    D_____
              S_____
          M_____
      S_____
T_____

In the exam you are often asked to give the
technical names of notes in a short passage.
Decide on the key and write out the scale.
Let's say that the passage is in F harmonic
minor ↘

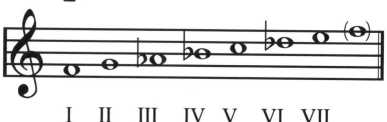

I   II   III   IV   V   VI   VII

Test yourself

Give the technical names of the notes [a] to [f] in the following passage. The key is Db major.

[a] _____ [b] _____ [c] _____

[d] _____ [e] _____ [f] _____

Name the key of this passage and write the technical names of the notes [a] to [f].

The key is _____

[a] _____ [b] _____ [c] _____

[d] _____ [e] _____ [f] _____

CHROMATIC SCALES

A chromatic scale is a thirteen note scale composed entirely of *semitones*.

When you write a chromatic scale you must put at least one note on each line and in each space, but not more than two notes. There is more than one way to write each scale as you can see from the following example for E♭ major. However, you usually do not change the subdominant or dominant notes.

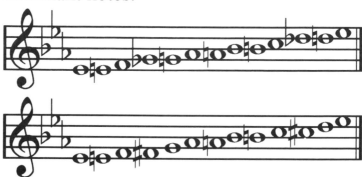

You could be asked to write a chromatic scale with or without key signature, in the treble, bass or alto clef, ascending, descending or both.

There are two variations of the chromatic scale: the harmonic and the melodic. At Grade 4 level you will **not** be asked for one or the other.

Since I prefer to follow simple rules, I shall describe the **harmonic chromatic scale**. You can then apply my rules and use the harmonic chromatic scale for all your answers.

The construction of the scale is identical for the major and minor key, both ascending and descending.

1. Put the key-note at both ends of the scale.
2. Write the *dominant* once only.
3. Put *two* notes on all the other lines and in all the other spaces.

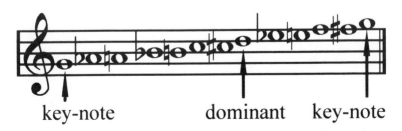

key-note   dominant   key-note

Test yourself

Write one octave of a chromatic scale,

1. ***without*** a key signature, ***ascending*** in semibreves and beginning on the given note.

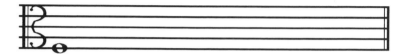

2. ***without*** a key signature, ***descending*** in semibreves, beginning on the given note.

3. ***with*** a key signature for C minor, ***ascending*** in semibreves, beginning on the dominant.

Teacher
Check
Time

TIME SIGNATURES

$\frac{4}{8}$ is the only new **simple** time signature for grade 4.

Students are sometimes confused between $\frac{2}{4}$ and $\frac{4}{8}$ time.   There is **no difference in notation** between pieces written in $\frac{2}{4}$ and $\frac{4}{8}$. The difference is in **how they are played**. In $\frac{2}{4}$ time the composer wants **two beats** in the bar. In $\frac{4}{8}$ time the piece should have **four beats** in the bar.

Here is a quick reminder of
simple time signatures:-

Duple →		$\frac{2}{4}$	$\frac{2}{2}$ or ¢
Triple →	$\frac{3}{8}$	$\frac{3}{4}$	$\frac{3}{2}$
Quadruple →	$\frac{4}{8}$	$\frac{4}{4}$ or C	$\frac{4}{2}$

Duplets

In simple time you met the triplet which divided a simple beat into 3 equal parts. Now you will meet the duplet. It is found in **compound time** when a **dotted beat** is divided into **2 equal parts**.

There are two ways of writing the duplet:-

1. Using dotted notes	2. Using a ² above the pair of notes
𝅝· = 𝅗𝅥· 𝅗𝅥·	𝅝· = 𝅗𝅥 𝅗𝅥
𝅗𝅥· = 𝅘𝅥· 𝅘𝅥·	𝅗𝅥· = 𝅘𝅥 𝅘𝅥
𝅘𝅥· = 𝅘𝅥· 𝅘𝅥𝅮	𝅘𝅥· = 𝅘𝅥 𝅘𝅥𝅮
𝅘𝅥𝅮· = 𝅘𝅥𝅮· 𝅘𝅥𝅯	𝅘𝅥𝅮· = 𝅘𝅥𝅮 𝅘𝅥𝅯

Double Dots

A single dot after a note lengthens it by half.	The second dot is worth half the first dot.

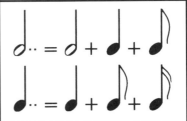

Try these:

Add the missing bar-lines to the following:

There are some new **compound time signatures** for Grade 4. You will not find them difficult because you mastered the principles of compound time in Grade 3.

Duple Time (2 dotted beats in a bar)

You will remember $\frac{6}{8}$ time. Six quavers in a bar gave **2 *dotted crotchet beats***.

Now we have $\frac{6}{4}$ and $\frac{6}{16}$ time.

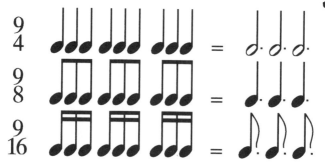

Triple Time (3 dotted beats)

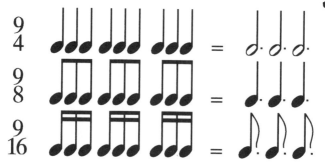

Quadruple Time (4 dotted beats)

Grouping Notes and Rests

Study again pages 32 to 38 in my Grade 3 book to revise the rules for the grouping of notes and rests.

The only difference with the compound times at Grade 4 level is that the note values are doubled for $\frac{6}{4}$ $\frac{9}{4}$ $\frac{12}{4}$ (crotchets instead of quavers) and halved for $\frac{6}{16}$ $\frac{9}{16}$ $\frac{12}{16}$ (semiquavers instead of quavers).

The Breve

We have already met the breve **rest** in Grade 3.   This is what it looks like:-

It is used to show a **_whole bar's rest_** in $\frac{4}{2}$.
Written as a **note** it looks like this:- 𝄎
It is worth two semibreves:-

𝄎 = 𝅝 + 𝅝

Test yourself

Rewrite this passage,
doubling the time values.

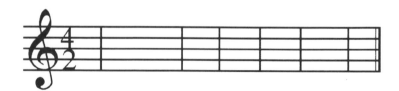

Test yourself

Add time signatures and
bar-lines where necessary.

Teacher
Check
Time

PRIMARY TRIADS AND CHORDS

Primary triads are formed on
the **tonic** - **I**
the **subdominant** - **IV**
the **dominant** - **V**

D Major

I   IV   V

D Minor

I   IV   V

Important

The dominant triad in a minor scale contains the leading note which needs to be raised a semitone.

Root, third (3rd) and fifth (5th) refer to the ***notes of a triad.*** Tonic (I), supertonic (II), mediant (III), subdominant (IV), dominant (V), submediant (VI) and leading note (VII) refer to the ***notes of a scale***.

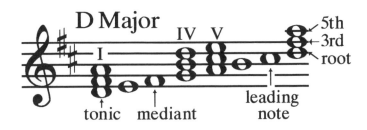

Write the tonic, subdominant and dominant triads of C **major** →

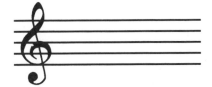

Write the tonic, subdominant and dominant triads of C **minor** *with key signature* →

Teacher Check Time

Primary Chords

In Grade 4 you could be asked to name chords that have been formed from the three primary triads. You do **not** have to write them. You only have to *recognise* them. This is easy because the *lowest* note of the **triad** - the **root** - is always at the *bottom* of the **chord** in Grade 4 questions.

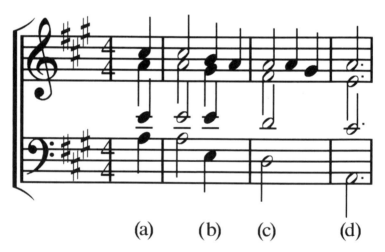

(a)   (b)   (c)   (d)

Name each of the chords (a) to (d) as tonic, subdominant or dominant.

(a) _____ (b) _____

(c) _____ (d) _____

INTERVALS

In my previous books you met **major, minor** and **perfect** intervals. Now in this Grade 4 book you will meet **augmented** and **diminished** intervals.

Augmented means BIGGER.
An augmented interval is one semitone *more* than a **major** interval or a **perfect** interval.

A **diminished** interval is SMALLER. It is one semitone *less* than a **minor** interval or one semitone *less* than a **perfect** interval.

Handy Hints

major + 1 semitone = augmented
perfect + 1 semitone = augmented
minor − 1 semitone = diminished
perfect − 1 semitone = diminished
major − 2 semitones = diminished

Here is a method to take the worry out of intervals so that you can always get the right answer! Follow these instructions:

Step by Step

1 Draw a piano keyboard:-

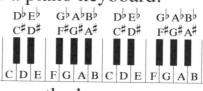

and name the keys

2 Find the lower note of the interval on the keyboard

3 Walk your fingers in semitone steps until you reach the upper note

4 Decide whether the interval is a 3rd, 4th, 5th, etc.

One Final Step

The chart on page 33 shows you how many semitones there are in each interval. Look at the chart to name the interval.

Interval Chart

Interval		Semitones
Perfect	8th	12
Augmented	7th	12
Major	7th	11
Minor	7th	10
Diminished	7th	9
Augmented	6th	10
Major	6th	9
Minor	6th	8
Diminished	6th	7
Augmented	5th	8
Perfect	5th	7
Diminished	5th	6
Augmented	4th	6
Perfect	4th	5
Diminished	4th	4
Augmented	3rd	5
Major	3rd	4
Minor	3rd	3
Diminished	3rd	2
Augmented	2nd	3
Major	2nd	2
Minor	2nd	1
Diminished	2nd	-

Test yourself

Use the chart on page 33
to find the following *intervals*:

_____   _____   _____

_____   _____   _____

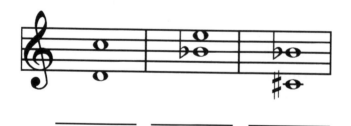

_____   _____   _____

Test yourself

Describe the *intervals* (a) to (e) in this passage:-

(a) _____

(b) _____

(c) _____

(d) _____

(e) _____

Teacher Check Time

MUSICAL
CROSSWORD

Clues Across

1. F minor has four of these.

5. A whole bar's rest in $\frac{4}{2}$ time.

6. B major has five of these.

8. Shorthand for *pianissimo*.

9. Musical term meaning *more*.

11. This lengthens a note by half.

13. A scale composed entirely of semitones.

Clues Down

1. Two letters for *loud then immediately soft*.

2. Two words meaning *in strict time*.

3. The name for a simple time like $\frac{3}{8}$.

4. A perfect 5th has seven of these.

7. You raise the 7th note in this minor scale.

10. Musical term meaning *very*.

12. The order of the first three flats.

ORNAMENTS

Many candidates 'run away' from facing ornaments. Don't be one of them. The correct playing of ornaments is so important to music that I'm sure you will want to make the effort to understand them. I shall take you through each one very carefully to give you confidence.

For each ornament at Grade 4 you have to be able to

1. **Recognise** the **sign**.
2. **Write** its name.
3. **Know** how it is **played**.

You will **not** have to write out the notes.

The Acciaccatura

It looks like this:- 𝅘𝅥   Acciaccatura is an Italian word meaning 'squeezed in'.

You play it as quickly as possible on the beat, just before you play the main note. We sometimes call the acciaccatura a 'short grace note'.

Note Values

Grace note: = a demisemiquaver

Main note: minus a demisemiquaver

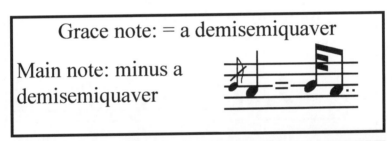

If the main note is longer than a crotchet:-	If the main note is dotted:-
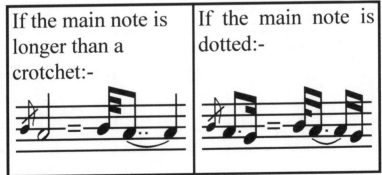	

The Appoggiatura

It looks like this:- ♪
It has **no line** through it.

The appogiatura takes
different values,
depending on the main note.

Note Values

If the main note is **not dotted**, the grace
note is **half** the value of the main note:

If the main note **is dotted**, the grace note
is **two thirds** the value of the main note:

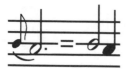 

The Double or Triple Appoggiatura

double →    triple →

Note Values

If the main note is *not dotted,* the grace note is *half* the value of the main note:	

If the main note *is dotted*, the grace note is *two thirds* the value of the main note:	

So far we have met two ornaments: the **acciaccatura** (**4** letter **c**'s) and the **appoggiatura** (**2 p**'s and **2 g**'s).

Test yourself

Write an acciaccatura before the notes marked with * Put them a note higher than the given note:-

Write an appoggiatura before each note →

Which do you think is the best way to play the following? Tick ✓ your choice in □:-

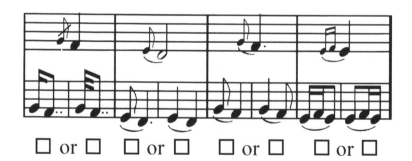

☐ or ☐   ☐ or ☐   ☐ or ☐   ☐ or ☐

The Arpeggio

 The wavy line tells you to ripple the chord in a harp-like manner from bottom to top. Arpeggio is Italian for harp-like.

When written, the notes take the smallest sensible value and are tied to the notes of the chord.

**Each note of the chord
is played in turn and held.**

The Upper Mordent

It looks like this →

and it is played like this →

1 The *main note*:
a demisemiquaver
2 The *note above*:
a demisemiquaver
3 The *main note*:
minus the two
demisemiquavers:-

When an upper
mordent is above a
minim, add an extra
tied crotchet:-

When the main note
is a dotted crotchet,
add an extra tied
quaver:-

The Lower Mordent

1 The *main note*:
   a demisemiquaver
2 The *note below*:
   a demisemiquaver
3 The *main note*:
   minus the two
   demisemiquavers:-
   It looks like this →

and it is played
like this →

Accidentals and Mordents

The accidental is written *above* the sign with an **upper** mordent and *below* the sign with a **lower** mordent. The *middle* note is given the accidental indicated.

The Upper Turn

It looks like this →

If *above* a *whole* note,
it is played like this:-

1. The *note above*
2. The *main note*
3. The *note below*
4. The *main note*

Divide the main note into 4 equal notes

If *after* a *whole* note,
    the *main* note   = *half* its value
    the *remainder* = 4 *equal* notes

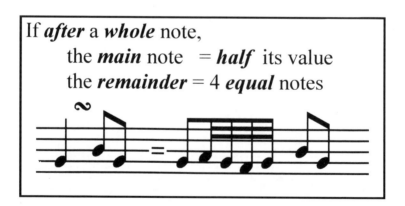

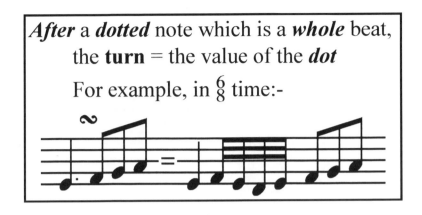

After a **dotted** note which is a **whole** beat, the **turn** = the value of the **dot**

For example, in ⁶⁄₈ time:-

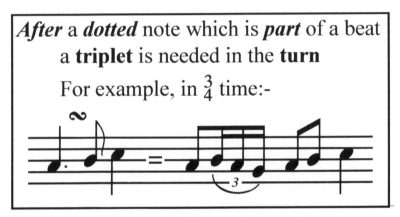

After a **dotted** note which is **part** of a beat a **triplet** is needed in the **turn**

For example, in ³⁄₄ time:-

Accidentals and Turns

Accidentals obey the **same** rules for turns as for mordents:-

 If **above** a turn they apply to the note **above**. If **below**, they apply to the note **below**

Test yourself

Put the sign for an **upper** mordent → above each note

← Put the sign for a **lower** mordent above each note

Put a ✓ in the □ showing the best way to play these mordents:-

□ or □   □ or □

Teacher
Check
Time

Test yourself

Put the sign for
an upper turn   →
above each note

Put the sign for
←   an upper turn
after each note

Put a ✓ in the □ showing the best way to
play these upper turns:-

□   or   □   □   or   □

□   or   □

The Trill or Shake

It looks like this:- *tr* or *tr* ~~~~
It is played with the **main note**
and the **note above**.
With early composers,
start a trill on the **note above**:-

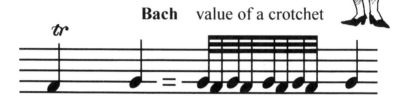

Bach   value of a crotchet

> Use semiquavers for **fast** pieces and
> demisemiquavers for **slower** pieces.

> If a **trill begins** with an **acciaccatura**,
> **start** on the note **above**.

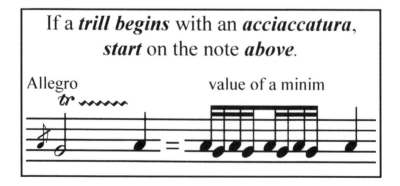

Allegro   value of a minim

With modern composers,
start a trill on the *main note*:-

Dvorak

Avoid repeated notes at the beginning or the end of a trill.   If this means adding an *extra* note, you will need a **triplet** before the last two notes of the trill (see above).

One Final Step

Grace notes are included in the trill.

Ready to test yourself?
Turn over →

Test yourself

Put the sign for
a trill or shake
above each note →

Put a ✓ in the □ to indicate the best way
to play these trills or shakes:-

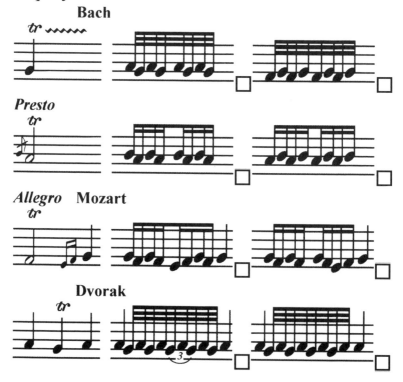

Name these ornament signs:

∿		∾	
♪		∿	
tr ∿∿∿		♪	

Write the signs for the ornaments:

	Upper turn
	Trill or Shake
	Lower mordent
	Appoggiatura
	Upper mordent
	Acciaccatura

Teacher Check Time

WORDS AND RHYTHM

At Grade 4 level you will be given a *choice* between writing a *four-bar rhythm or* writing a *rhythm to words*.

In my Theory is Fun Grade 3 book you met four-bar rhythms and these four characters:

In this Grade 4 book we shall look at writing a rhythm to words.

Handy Hints
on Words and Rhythm

1 A musical phrase is often *four* bars in length. For example:-

Rhythm:

$\frac{6}{8}$

Words: So | big was Bronto | saurus that one | brain was not e | nough.

         *   *

2 Put bar-lines in front of important syllables. (See * in above example)

3 Choose a time signature. Consider $\frac{6}{8}$ time since it combines duple time and the possibility of dividing a beat into 3.

4 Do *not* join notes. Write each note separately for each syllable.

One Final Step →

Test yourself

Compose rhythms for the following words.

1 Give thought, now, to the dinosaurs,
Whom no-one fears today.

rhythm _____

words ....

rhythm _____

words ....

2 Whenever you look at moon and stars,
Whenever the wind is wild.

rhythm _____

words ....

rhythm _____

words ....

Four-Bar Rhythms

Write a four-bar rhythm for Pablo, Bonita and Carlos.   Begin with an anacrusis (see Theory is Fun Grade 3 page 50).

$\frac{4}{4}$ _____

_____

GENERAL QUESTIONS

You will be presented with a passage of music and asked questions about it. All the following points (mentioned on pages 56-57 of my Grade 3 book) are relevant when dealing with this section at Grade 4:-

Musical terms	Key signatures
Tonic triads	Degrees of a scale
Intervals	Naming notes
Note values	Time signatures

In addition to the topics covered in Grade 3, there will be questions on new topics in Grade 4.

There will probably be simple questions on orchestral instruments. You will need to know the family group of each instrument and the clefs which are used.

INSTRUMENTS OF THE ORCHESTRA

Instrument	treble	alto	tenor	bass
violin	●			
viola		●		
cello	(●)		(●)	●
double bass				●
flute	●			
oboe	●			
bassoon			(●)	●
clarinet	●			
trumpet	●			
horn	●			●
trombone			(●)	●
tuba				●

(●) this clef is sometimes used. Knowledge of the tenor clef is not expected until Grade 5.

A note about notes

String instruments can play more than one note at a time - sometimes two, three or even four notes. Wind instruments can play only one note at a time.

The String Family

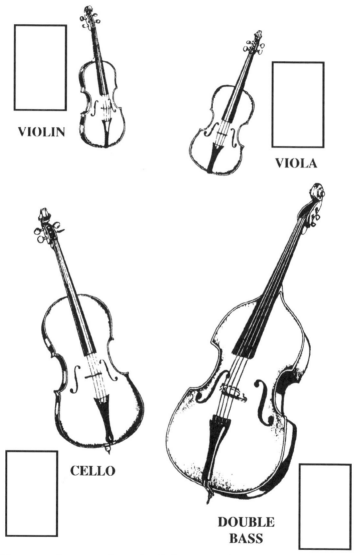

VIOLIN

VIOLA

CELLO

DOUBLE BASS

Draw the main clef for each instrument.

The Woodwind Family

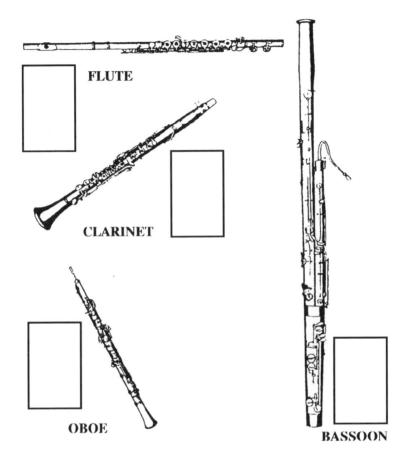

FLUTE

CLARINET

OBOE

BASSOON

In each box draw the main clef for the instrument.

The Brass Family

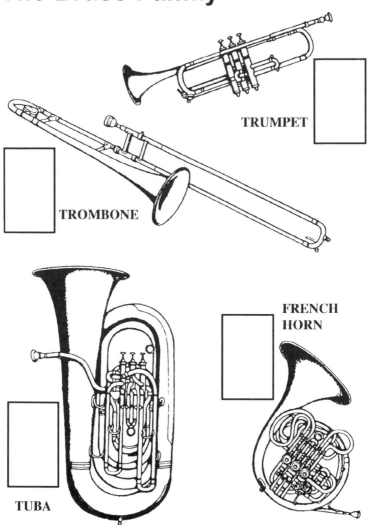

TRUMPET

TROMBONE

FRENCH HORN

TUBA

Draw the main clef for each instrument.

The Percussion Family

TIMPANI **CYMBALS**

Some members of the
percussion family
contribute to the
rhythm and dynamics
of a piece of music.
Others can play notes
at varying pitch.

We shall look more
closely at this family
in the Grade 5 book.

Performance Directions

Brass and string instruments can use a mute to play quietly.

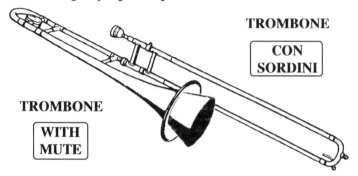

The term *senza sordini* tells you to play without a mute.

To a violinist, ⌐ means 'down' bow and V means 'up' bow.   Here are some other directions for string players:

play on the G string	*sul G*
play near the bridge	*sul ponticello*
pluck the strings	*pizzicato*
play with the bow	*arco*

You will find a list of the important general musical signs on pages 76 and 77.

Test yourself

Name the family for each instrument.

1. violin   _____
2. oboe   _____
3. trombone _____
4. bassoon   _____
5. clarinet   _____
6. tuba   _____

Name the main clef for each instrument.

7. cello   _____
8. clarinet   _____
9. flute   _____
10. trumpet   _____
11. tuba   _____
12. viola   _____

Check your answers

Musical terms wordsearch

I	B	A	S	O	P	R	A	E	S
A	R	W	O	U	K	A	C	Y	A
X	A	E	T	X	I	O	R	B	N
Y	L	Q	T	G	L	Y	Q	V	S
M	E	H	O	E	L	U	I	S	N
E	N	C	V	G	N	P	Z	K	I
Q	T	K	B	G	I	U	S	T	O
Y	I	F	V	F	V	O	Q	X	M
O	R	O	N	O	S	B	G	I	G
H	B	X	B	V	Y	I	P	E	U

CLUES

1. Slow down
2. Held back
3. Exact, proper
4. With rich tone
5. Without

6. Above
7. Below
8. Swift
9. Less
10. Little

A DICTIONARY OF MUSICAL TERMS

GRADE 4

AND A LIST OF SIGNS

A (à) - at, to, by, for, in the style of
Accelerando - becoming gradually faster
Adagietto - rather slow
Adagio - slow, leisurely
Adagissimo - very slow
Affetuoso - tenderly
Affrettando - hurrying
Agitato - agitated
Alla - in the style of
Alla marcia - in the style of a march
Alla polacca - in the style of a Polonaise
Allargando - broadening out
Allegretto - slightly slower than allegro
Allegro - lively, reasonably fast
Allegro assai - very quick
Amabile - amiable, pleasant
Andante - at a walking pace
Andantino - a little slower or
   a little faster than andante
Animato - lively, animated
Animé - animated, lively
Appassionata - with passion
Assai - very
Assez - enough, sufficiently

Attacca - go on immediately
A tempo - resume the normal speed
Avec - with
Bravura - with boldness and spirit
Brillante - sparkling, brilliant
Cantabile - in a singing style
Cantando - in a singing style
Cédez - yield, relax the speed
Col; Con - with
Con anima - with deep feeling - soul
Con brio - with vigour
Con moto - with movement
Con spirito - with spirit, life, energy
Crescendo [cresc.] - gradually louder
Da capo [D.C.] - from the beginning
Dal segno [D.S.] - repeat from the sign ৡ
Deciso - with determination
Decrescendo [decresc.] - gradually softer
Delicato - delicately
Diminuendo [dim.] - gradually softer
Dolce - sweetly
Dolcissimo - very sweetly
Dolente - sadly
Dolore - grief, sorrow

Doppio - double
Doppio movimento - double the speed
Douce - sweet
En dehors - prominent
Energico - with energy
Espressione - expression
Espressivo [Espress., Espr.] - with expression, feeling
Et - and
Facile - easy
Fortepiano [fp] - loud, then immediately soft
Fine - the end
Forte [f] - loud
Fortissimo [ff] - very loud
Forza - force, power
Forzando [fz] - with a strong accent
Fuoco - fire
Furioso - furiously
Giocoso - merry
Giusto - exact, proper
Grandioso - in a grand manner
Grave - very slow
Grazioso - gracefully

Lacrimoso - tearfully
Largamente - in a broad style
Larghetto - faster than largo
Largo - slow & stately, broad
Legatissimo - as smoothly as possible
Legato - smoothly
Légèrement - lightly
Leggiero - lightly
Lent - slow
Lento - slowly
L'Istesso - the same
Ma - but

Ma non troppo - but not too much
Maestoso - majestically
Mais - but
Marcato - marked, accented
Martellato - hammered out
Marziale - in a military style
Meno - less
Meno mosso - less movement
Mesto - sadly
Mezzo forte [mf] - moderately loud
Mezzo piano [mp] - moderately soft
Misterioso - mysteriously

Moderato - at a moderate pace
Modéré - at a moderate speed
Moins - less
Molto - much
Morendo - dying away
Mosso - movement
Moto - movement
Movimento - movement
Niente - nothing
Nobilmente - nobly
Non - not
Non tanto - not so much
Non troppo - not too much
Parlando - in a speaking manner
Parlante - in a speaking manner
Pastorale - in a pastoral style
Patetico - with feeling
Perdendosi - dying away
Pesante - heavily
Peu - little
Pianissimo [pp] - very soft
Piano [p] - soft
Piu - more
Pizzicato [pizz.] - plucked

Plus - more
Poco a poco - little by little
Possibile - possible
    Presto possibile - as fast as possible
Presser - hurry
    En pressant - hurrying on
Prestissimo - as fast as possible
Presto - very quick
Quasi - as if, resembling
Ralentir - slow down
Rallentando [rall.] - becoming
    gradually slower
Retenu - held back
    En retenant - holding back
Risoluto - boldly
Ritardando [ritard. rit.] - gradually
    slower
Ritenuto [riten. rit.] - hold back,
    slower at once
Ritmico - rhythmically
Sans - without
Scherzando - playfully
Scherzo - a joke
Semplice - simple

Sempre - always
Senza - without
Sforzando [sf, sfz] - with a sudden accent
Simile [Sim.] - in the same way
Slargando - gradually slower
Slentando - gradually slower
Smorzando - dying away
Sonoro - with rich tone
Sopra - above
Sospirando - sighing
Sostenuto - sustained
Sotto - below

    Sotto voce - in an undertone
Spiritoso - lively, animated
Staccatissimo - very detached
Staccato - short, detached
Stringendo - gradually faster
Subito - suddenly
Tanto - so much
Tempo - speed, time
Tempo comodo - at a comfortable speed
Tempo primo - resume the original
    speed

Tempo rubato - with some freedom of time

Tenuto - held on

Tranquillo - quietly

Très - very

Tristamente, Triste - sad, sorrowful

Troppo - too much

Tutti - all

Veloce - swift

Vibrato - vibrating

Vif - lively

Vite - quick

Vivace, Vivo - lively, quick

Vivacissimo - very lively

Voce - voice

Volta - time

    Prima volta - first time

    Seconda volta - second time

Volti subito [V.S.] - turn the page quickly

A LIST OF MUSICAL SIGNS

⌢ ⌣ - pause on the note

\> - accent the note

♩ - accent the note strongly

< - becoming louder

> - becoming softer

<> - becoming louder then softer

𝄇 - repeat

♩ = 60 - 60 crotchet beats in a
minute

♩ - accent and separate the note
slightly

♩♩♩ - semi-staccato

♪ 𝆑 - staccato [short, detached] =
dot over or under note

♪ 𝆒 - super-staccato [staccatissimo]

⌒ - slur (over a group of notes)
play the notes smoothly

8va ⌐⎯⎯⎯⎤
8 ⌐----------⌐ - play an octave higher

8va ⎯⎯⎯⎯⌐
8 ----------⌐ - play an octave lower

♪ - appoggiatura

♪ - acciaccatura (grace or
crushed note)

∾ - upper turn

ᴡ ᴪ - upper and lower mordent

𝆕 or 𝆕∿∿ - trill or shake

{ - arpeggio

THE NEXT STEP?

THEORY IS FUN

GRADE 5

Maureen Cox

> **THEORY IS FUN
> GRADE 5**

all key signatures to 7 sharps or flats; tenor clef and scales; compound intervals: major, minor, perfect, diminished and augmented; irregular time signatures, quintuple & septuple; tonic, supertonic subdominant & dominant chords; writing at concert pitch; short & open score; orchestral instruments in detail; composing a melody for instrument or voice; perfect, imperfect & plagal cadences; more musical terms, including German.

ISBN 0 9516940 9 X

Where are **you** going?

To get my
**THEORY IS FUN
GRADE 5**

PROGRESS CHART

Key Signatures ○
The Alto Clef ○
Major and Minor Scales ○
Technical Names ○
Chromatic Scales ○
Time Signatures ○
Primary Triads and Chords ○
Intervals ○
Ornaments ○
Words and Rhythm ○
General Questions ○
Instruments of the Orchestra ○
Dictionary of Musical Terms ○
List of Signs ○

NAME: